anythink

CIRCLE
A COOKIE OR THE SUN IN THE SKY

By SYDNEY LEPEW

Illustrated by ANNIE WILKENSON

CANTATA
LEARNING

MANKATO, MINNESOTA

WWW.CANTATALEARNING.COM

CANTATA LEARNING

MANKATO, MINNESOTA

Published by Cantata Learning
1710 Roe Crest Drive
North Mankato, MN 56003
www.cantatalearning.com

Library of Congress Control Number: 2014957002
978-1-63290-273-3 (hardcover/CD)
978-1-63290-425-6 (paperback/CD)
978-1-63290-467-6 (paperback)

Circle: A Cookie or the Sun in the Sky by Sydney LePew
Illustrated by Annie Wilkinson

Book design, Tim Palin Creative
Editorial direction, Flat Sole Studio
Executive musical production and direction, Elizabeth Draper
Music produced by Wes Schuck
Audio recorded, mixed, and mastered at Two Fish Studios, Mankato, MN

Printed in the United States of America.

VISIT
WWW.CANTATALEARNING.COM/ACCESS-OUR-MUSIC
TO SING ALONG TO THE SONG

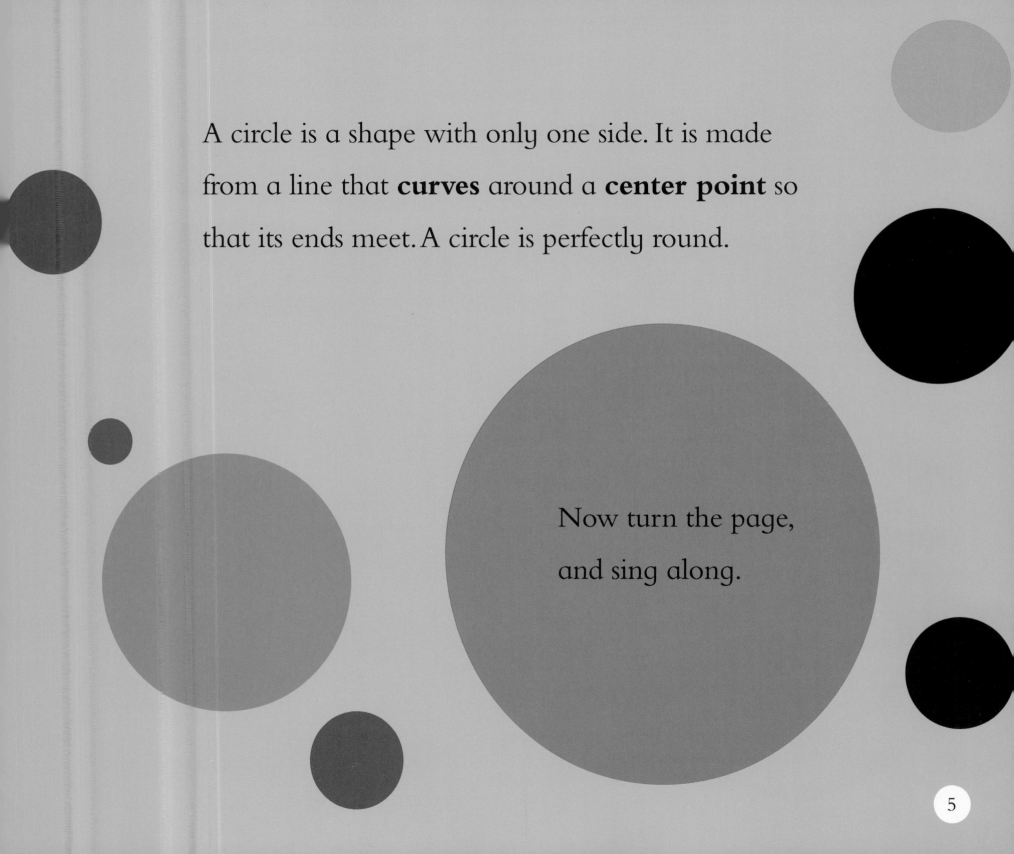

A circle is a shape with only one side. It is made from a line that **curves** around a **center point** so that its ends meet. A circle is perfectly round.

Now turn the page, and sing along.

Circles all around us,
and circles are round.

Circles all around us,
and circles are round.

A circle is the sun up in the sky
shining down as we play outside,
and it's the ball we kick up high.

A circle is the cookie that you just ate.

It's the roundness of your plate,

and the clock that says it's getting late.

Circles all around us,
and circles are round.

Circles all around us,
and circles are round.

A circle is a snowman's eye,

a snowball for a snowball fight.

And a **puck** sliding across the ice.

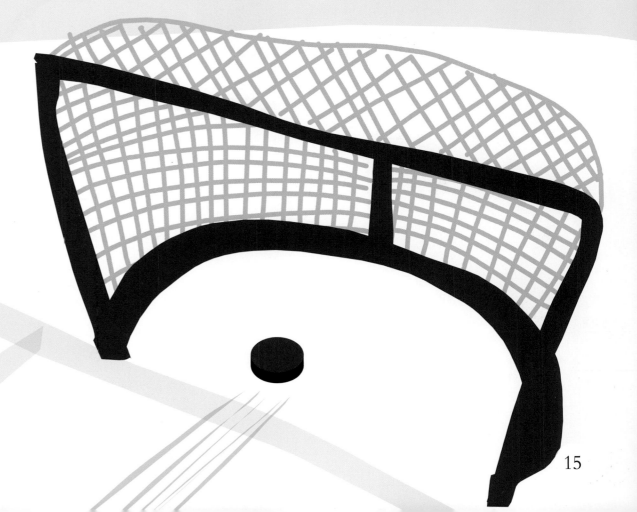

Want to draw a circle? It's easy.

Just put a dot in the middle of your paper.

Draw a line that curves around that point.

Keep going until the ends of the line meet!

owl
only
old
onion
on
own
oak
off

10
100
1000
10,000
100,0
1,000
10,000

18

A circle is the number zero.

It's the small letter o.

Even Earth is a circle, you know!

Circles all around us,
and circles are round.

Circles all around us,
and circles are round.

SONG LYRICS
Circle: A Cookie or the Sun in the Sky

Circles all around us,
and circles are round.

Circles all around us,
and circles are round.

A circle is the sun up in the sky
shining down as we play outside,
and it's the ball we kick up high.

A circle is the cookie that you just ate.
It's the roundness of your plate,
and the clock that says it's getting late.

Circles all around us,
and circles are round.

Circles all around us,
and circles are round.

A circle is a snowman's eye,
a snowball for a snowball fight.
And a puck sliding across the ice.

Want to draw a circle? It's easy.
Just put a dot in the middle of
    your paper.

Draw a line that curves around
    that point.
Keep going until the ends of the
    line meet!

A circle is the number zero.
It's the small letter o.
Even Earth is a circle, you know!

Circles all around us,
and circles are round.

Circles all around us,
and circles are round.

Folk
Wes Schuck

Circle: A Cookie or the Sun in the Sky

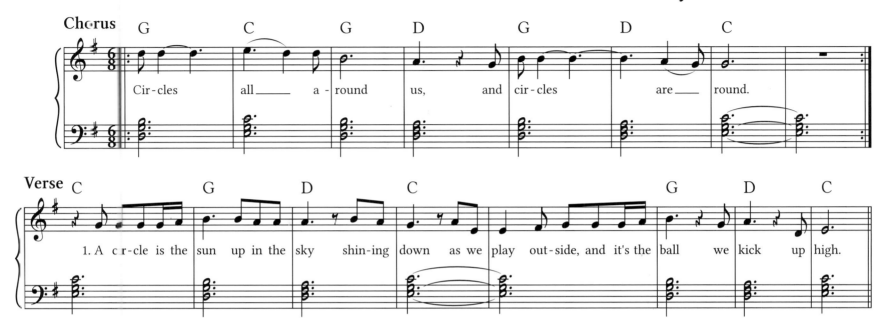

Chorus

Cir-cles all____ a-round us, and cir-cles are____ round.

Verse

1. A cir-cle is the sun up in the sky shin-ing down as we play out-side, and it's the ball we kick up high.

Verse 2
A circle is the cookie that you just ate.
It's the roundness of your plate,
and the clock that says it's getting late.

Chorus

Verse 3
A circle is a snowman's eye,
a snowball for a snowball fight.
And a puck sliding across the ice.

Spoken
Want to draw a circle? It's easy.
Just put a dot in the middle of your paper.
Draw a line that curves around that point.
Keep going until the ends of the line meet!

Verse 4
A circle is the number zero.
It's the small letter o.
Even Earth is a circle, you know!

Chorus

GLOSSARY

center point—the spot in the middle of a circle

curves—bends around

puck—a black rubber disk that is used to play hockey

GUIDED READING ACTIVITIES

1. How many circles are in your classroom or bedroom?

2. Practice drawing a circle. Now use your circle to draw something else. What did you draw? A bicycle? A person? An apple hanging from a tree?

3. List the circles you found in this book.

TO LEARN MORE

Aboff, Marcie. *If You Were a Circle.* Minneapolis, MN: Picture Window Books, 2010.

Brocket, Jane. *Circles, Stars, and Squares: Looking for Shapes.* Minneapolis: Millbrook Press, 2013.

Corcorane, Ann. *Circles Everywhere.* Mankato, MN: Capstone Press, 2012.

Lawrence, Elizabeth. *I See Circles.* New York: Cavendish Square Publishing, 2015.